Kids' Guide

BIGGEST ECONOMIES IN *Asia*

Dream big, our little Boo

– Mommy & Daddy –

BIGGEST ECONOMIES

in *Asia*

Little Explorers' Guide to Asia's Leading
Industries and the Stories Behind Their Rise!

By Yeonsil Yoo

Contents

Part 1. East Asia

Part 2. Southeast Asia

Part 3. South Asia

Bangladesh: The Fabric Genius
India: The Code Masters
Pakistan: The Cotton Expert
Sri Lanka: The Tea Haven

Part 4. Central Asia

Kazakhstan: The Energy Explorer
Uzbekistan: The Hidden Wonders Seeker

Part 5. West Asia (Middle East)

Iran: The Daring Energy Detectives
Israel: The Tech Stars
Saudi Arabia: The King of Oil
Turkey: The Car Craftsmen
United Arab Emirates: The Sky-Scraping Sculptors

WELCOME TO *Asia*

LAND OF BOOMING ECONOMIES & INSPIRING STORIES!

Hello, future world traveler! By opening this book, you've taken the first step on an exciting journey across Asia—a continent bursting with vibrant cultures, age-old traditions, and yes, booming economies.

You might be thinking, 'what exactly is an economy?' Think of it as a giant marketplace where people create, buy, and sell all kinds of things. It's a showcase of a nation's wealth and achievements!

As you flip through the pages, you'll explore various Asian countries, each with its own unique economic tale to tell. Be prepared to discover heaps of cool facts and unravel the fascinating histories behind major industries in each nation.

Are you ready? Let's grab an explorer's hat and start the adventure now!

MAP OF ASIA

Part 1. East Asia

CHINA

The Land of Countless Inventions

- POPULATION: 1.4 BILLION
- CAPITAL: BEIJING
- OFFICIAL LANGUAGE: CHINESE (MANDARIN)

Imagine a country with more people than all of Canada, the United States, and Mexico combined—that's China!

China is known as "the world's factory" because it makes more stuff than any other country on earth. But it wasn't always that way. For a long time, China's economy used to be quite isolated.

That all changed in 1978 when China's leader, Deng Xiaoping, rolled out a game-changing plan called "Reform and Opening-Up." With so many people and new ideas flowing in, China's factories began to buzz with activity.

Today, these factories create all sorts of things: from toys and clothes to cutting-edge gadgets. Next time you pick up a toy or use a device, check for a "Made in China" label. If you spot one, you've got a piece of China's incredible story right in your hands!

Japan

The Robot Wonderland

- **Population:** 123 million
- **Capital:** Tokyo
- **Official Language:** Japanese

Did you ever wish for a robot buddy to tidy up your toys or play games with you? In Japan, it's not just a wish—it's reality!

After World War II, Japan's economy began to boom. Soon, they faced challenges like labor shortages, but they also saw amazing opportunities in technology. To tackle these challenges and seize the opportunities, Japan decided to invest big-time in making robots. In the 1980s, they launched a project aimed at creating intelligent machines, taking their robot technology to the next level!

Today, Japan has more robots per person than almost every other country. Japanese robots can be found doing all kinds of jobs, like taking orders, delivering food, or even dancing!

So the next time you see a robot out in the world, think of Japan. It's where robot buddies aren't just dreams—they're part of everyday life. How awesome is that?

SOUTH KOREA

The Cool Pop Culture Creator

- POPULATION: 52 MILLION
- CAPITAL: SEOUL
- OFFICIAL LANGUAGE: KOREAN

Ever grooved to a catchy K-pop song or watched a thrilling K-drama on TV? These are just a couple of the entertainment products produced by a small country with a big imagination—South Korea!

Back in the 1990s, South Korea decided to pour a lot of love and effort into creating incredible music, TV shows, and movies. They sparked a cultural movement called 'Hallyu' (or Korean wave) that swept over Asia. By the time the 2010s rolled around, K-pop tunes and K-dramas were catching the hearts of people not just in Asia but all over the world!

Thanks to global streaming platforms like Netflix or Spotify, people in over 190 different countries can access Korean art and culture as soon as it's released! It's a tale of how a small country dreamt big, used creativity and passion, and ended up spreading joy worldwide. Isn't that amazing?

TAIWAN

The Tiny Chip Superhero

- POPULATION: 23 MILLION
- CAPITAL: TAIPEI
- OFFICIAL LANGUAGE: CHINESE (MANDARIN)

What if I told you that a tiny island nation in the Pacific Ocean called Taiwan makes one of the smallest, but most important products on Earth? They're called semiconductor chips, and act as the mini command centers for all your electronic gadgets, including your computer, your phone, and even your refrigerator!

Back in the 1980s, Taiwan's researchers and leaders got together and hatched an ingenious plan. They aimed to become the best semiconductor chip-makers in the world. To do this, they created special zones for tech companies and invested heavily in research and education. Today, those special zones are at the heart of the world's semiconductor industry!

So next time your favorite game loads without a hitch or your video call goes perfectly, remember it's thanks to the tiny chip superheroes from Taiwan, the hidden heroes of our tech world!

Part 2. Southeast Asia

INDONESIA

The Island of Plenty

- POPULATION: 279 MILLION
- CAPITAL: JAKARTA
- OFFICIAL LANGUAGE: INDONESIAN

Love crunchy cereal or delicious tropical fruits? There's a good chance your favorite foods grew under the warm sun of Indonesia!

After World War II, Indonesia needed to import rice and other common foods from other countries. But in the 1970s, the government built irrigation canals, invested in fertilizers and pesticides, and taught farmers new methods to grow crops.

With hard work and innovation, Indonesia began producing lots of its own rice! Today, Indonesia is known for more than just its rice. They're also major producers of corn, sugarcane, and even palm oil!

So, when you enjoy cereal or fruits at your breakfast table, remember they're not just tasty treats. They're delicious pieces of a big dream, made real by Indonesia's determination and smart farming!

MALAYSIA

The Master of Electronics

- POPULATION: 34 MILLION
- CAPITAL: KUALA LUMPUR
- OFFICIAL LANGUAGE: MALAY

Did you know that Malaysia is really good at making electronics like tiny transistors and clever circuits? For a long time, this industrious country has been making the parts that help our electronic devices work like magic!

But how did Malaysia become so important to the electronics industry? Well, in the late 20th century, Malaysia's smart leaders changed some rules to welcome big tech companies from around the world. They set up factories and hired people in Malaysia.

Thanks to these early investments and their skilled workers, Malaysia has become a home of electronic champions.

So the next time you hear your phone ringing or see a message pop up on your screen, remember that it's all thanks to Malaysia. They are the unsung heroes, silently powering our daily tech magic!

PHILIPPINES

Global Teamwork Champions

- POPULATION: 116 MILLION
- CAPITAL: MANILA
- OFFICIAL LANGUAGES: FILIPINO AND ENGLISH

Do you like working with your friends on school projects? The Philippines loves it too!

This country is like a giant team that supports work globally. Companies call this "Business Process Outsourcing," but that's just a fancy name for super teamwork!

Back in the 1990s, the Philippines had a brainwave. They realized they had a pool of talented, English-speaking people who could solve problems remotely by using computers. Today, they've become so skilled at it that they handle over 10% of the world's outsourced work! A massive high-five to that!

When you're collaborating with your friends on a school project, remember the Philippines: they turned teamwork into a global success! Just imagine the big things your little team could achieve too!

SINGAPORE

The Little Island With a Giant Harbor

- POPULATION: 6 MILLION
- CAPITAL: SINGAPORE
- OFFICIAL LANGUAGES: ENGLISH, CHINESE (MANDARIN), MALAY, AND TAMIL

Singapore is a tiny island that is only large enough to hold a single city. But did you know it's one of the biggest ports in the world?

Singapore has the perfect spot right in the middle of busy sea routes that connect the East and the West. This fantastic location has made it a favorite stopping point for ships traveling between Europe and Asia for hundreds of years. With Asia's economies booming in the 20th century, Singapore's port became the busiest you could imagine.

Today, it's such a bustling hub that it handles a huge chunk of all the world's shipping containers!

This little, but mighty island shows us that no matter how small you are, with some smart thinking and hard work, you can make a big splash in the world! So remember, you can do the same!

THAILAND

The Dreamy Vacation Kingdom

- POPULATION: 70 MILLION
- CAPITAL: BANGKOK
- OFFICIAL LANGUAGE: THAI

Have you ever dreamt of sunny beaches, tasty food, and super friendly people? That's Thailand! It's a country that is always ready to throw a fun party with its visitors.

Back in the 1960s, Thailand was mostly focused on farming. But then the country's leaders had a bright idea! Their beautiful nature and amazing culture could attract people from all over the world. So, they started building better roads, fancy hotels, and awesome tourist spots! This turned places like Bangkok, Phuket, and Chiang Mai into must-visit destinations for travelers.

Today, Thailand is a top tourist attraction with over 35 million visitors every year! That's enough people to fill 500 HUGE stadiums! And here's more—every yummy dish you eat, or souvenir you buy, helps Thailand continue to grow and protect its stunning natural beauty. Now that's a tasty way to make a difference!

VIETNAM

The Assembly Whiz

- POPULATION: 105 MILLION
- CAPITAL: HANOI
- OFFICIAL LANGUAGE: VIETNAMESE

Do you like solving puzzles? Vietnam does too! But instead of jigsaw pieces, they use lots of little parts to create things like clothes, shoes, and toys!

For a long time, Vietnam mainly focused on farming. But when the cost of production rose in China, companies began looking for new places to make their goods. Vietnam seized this opportunity with open arms! Thanks to its young, eager workforce and a business-friendly environment, many international firms moved their factories to Vietnam. This shift brought in more money, introduced new technologies, and strengthened Vietnam's trade relationships with other nations.

Now, Vietnam is a global manufacturing powerhouse! By using smaller pieces and smart choices, Vietnam assembled itself into something incredible! So remember, just like a puzzle, when you put the right pieces together with some effort, you can create something truly amazing!

Part 3. South Asia

BANGLADESH

The Fabric Genius

- POPULATION: 167 MILLION
- CAPITAL: DHAKA
- OFFICIAL LANGUAGE: BENGALI

Ever wondered how clothes are made? They start with large squares of fabric, like the soft cotton in your t-shirt. Think of fabric as pizza dough—it's the base for every delicious combination you can imagine!

Long ago, Dhaka, now the capital of Bangladesh, was famous for its super-soft muslin that was loved by kings, queens, and traders worldwide. Though the special technique for making Dhaka muslin has mostly been lost, Bangladesh has kept its textile traditions alive in other beautiful fabrics.

Today, Bangladesh mixes its textile heritage with new technology from all over the world as one of the top fabric producers in the world. Next time you're wearing your favorite t-shirt, check its tag. There's a good chance it comes from Bangladesh, where ancient craft meets the modern world!

INDIA

The Code Masters

- POPULATION: 1.4 BILLION
- CAPITAL: NEW DELHI
- OFFICIAL LANGUAGES: HINDI, ENGLISH, AND 21 OTHER RECOGNIZED LANGUAGES

Do you love playing games or using fun apps on your tablet or phone? Guess what? Many of those were made by coding wizards from India!

After leaving the British Empire and becoming its own country, India invested heavily in educating its people in science and technology. They set up special schools, called Indian Institutes of Technology (IITs), to train super-smart scientists and engineers. As the world became more digital, India had lots of talented people ready to create cool programs for everyday use. It wasn't long before companies all over the world were seeking help from India!

Today, many kids in India dream of becoming engineers and programmers, hoping to make a positive difference in our world. Just think—with some coding skills and a dash of imagination, you too could create something that people around the globe will adore!

PAKISTAN

The Cotton Expert

- POPULATION: 248 MILLION
- CAPITAL: ISLAMABAD
- OFFICIAL LANGUAGES: ENGLISH AND URDU

I bet you've got a big bag of soft fluffy white puffs in your bathroom. Those are cotton balls, and that's what the fabric in your t-shirt or bedsheets looks like before it is turned to fabric. Pakistan is a superstar when it comes to growing these tiny clouds of joy!

Way back, many thousands of years ago, before Pakistan was called Pakistan, there was a place called the Indus Valley Civilization. And the people who lived there were master cotton growers! They passed their knowledge down from parent to child through time. The result? Pakistan is the fifth-largest cotton producer in the world!

Only the massive countries of India, China, the USA and Brazil produce more (and they all have way more land to grow on!) What's the secret to Pakistan's cottony success? Loads of sunshine, rich soil, and centuries-old farming know-how. Every time you put on a soft t-shirt, think of it as a high-five from Pakistan!

Sri Lanka

The Tea Haven

- POPULATION: 23 MILLION
- CAPITAL: SRI JAYAWARDENEPURA KOTTE
- OFFICIAL LANGUAGES: SINHALA AND TAMIL

Do you like sipping on a warm cup of tea on a cold winter day? Or maybe an icy sweet tea on the beach is more your style? However you take it, Sri Lanka might have been behind your delightful moment!

A long time ago, Sri Lanka was all about coffee. But a plant disease nicknamed "Devastating Emily" wiped out their coffee crops. Seeing his coffee dreams crumble, a Scottish planter named James Taylor had an idea. He introduced tea plants as an experiment to one of his fields, and guess what? It was a roaring success!

Today, this tiny island in the Indian Ocean is a top-five tea producing nation. Whenever you're having a cozy cup of tea, picture it starting its journey from the lush hills of Sri Lanka. What a tea-riffic tale, right?

Part 4. Central Asia

KAZAKHSTAN

The Energy Explorer

- POPULATION: 19 MILLION
- CAPITAL: ASTANA
- OFFICIAL LANGUAGES: KAZAKH AND RUSSIAN

Have you ever imagined yourself as a brave adventurer, seeking buried treasure? That's exactly what Kazakhstan does, but they're not hunting for gold or jewels—their treasure is oil and gas!

Oil and gas are like magic potions that power up cars, run our factories, and even heat our homes. Deep within Kazakhstan lies one of the world's largest oilfields, called the Tengiz Field. Kazakhstan works with companies from all over the world to find new ways of digging up this valuable treasure, making them a giant in the energy industry.

The next time you feel the purr of a car engine or bask in the warmth of your home, remember, you might be experiencing the fruits of Kazakhstan's incredible energy hunt. It's a thrilling tale of a nation's knack for adventure turning nature's gift into the world's energy!

UZBEKISTAN

The Hidden Wonders Seeker

- POPULATION: 31 MILLION
- CAPITAL: TASHKENT
- OFFICIAL LANGUAGE: UZBEK

Ever heard of uranium? It's a special kind of rock that can be used to create lots of energy! And guess where you can find lots of it? Uzbekistan!

A long time ago, Uzbekistan was part of a big group of countries known as the Soviet Union. They all worked together to find special things in the earth, like uranium. When they discovered that Uzbekistan had lots of these special rocks, they brought in big machines to help collect them.

Even though the group of countries doesn't work together like before, Uzbekistan still uses the machines and knowledge they learned to find uranium. And guess what? Uzbekistan is one of the top ten producers of uranium worldwide. Imagine, a rock from Uzbekistan might be helping to power your home! Isn't it incredible?

Part 5. West Asia (Middle East)

IRAN

The Daring Energy Detectives

- POPULATION: 89 MILLION
- CAPITAL: TEHRAN
- OFFICIAL LANGUAGE: PERSIAN

You already know how oil and gas keep our daily lives going, right? Well, it's not just one country providing all that energy—it's a team effort! And one of the superstars in this energy game is Iran!

Back in 1908, a daring British entrepreneur named William Knox D'Arcy, set out on an epic journey through Iran. He and his team were looking for 'liquid gold'—a fun nickname they came up with for oil! Iran is a difficult country to explore, because it has vast deserts and rugged terrain. Trying to find oil was like a big game of hide and seek. But here's the catch: they never gave up, and with persistence they struck oil in a remote place called Masjed Soleiman.

Nowadays, Iran produces millions of barrels of oil for sale throughout Asia. Remember that when things seem super hard, keep searching for a solution, because sometimes the most amazing treasures are hiding in the sneakiest spots!

ISRAEL

The Tech Stars

- POPULATION: 9.2 MILLION
- CAPITAL: JERUSALEM
- OFFICIAL LANGUAGES: HEBREW

Have you ever come up with a cool new solution for a problem? One that no one has thought of before? That's something Israel does really well, too. In fact, there are so many bright minds bursting with new ideas in Israel that it's often called the 'Startup Nation' because of how many new companies are solving tough challenges!

But why is Israel such a startup superstar? It's not just their daring spirit and knack for innovation. It's also their culture! In Israel, people are encouraged to ask tough questions about everything, to be curious, to always keep learning and to never give up. When someone tries something new and it doesn't work, they just dust themselves off and try again!

It's OK to think outside the box, just like Israel. Maybe your favorite game or a helpful app on your parents' phone was invented by an Israeli startup! Be bold, be brave, be innovative—just like Israel's tech stars!

SAUDI ARABIA

The King of Oil

- POPULATION: 36 MILLION
- CAPITAL: RIYADH
- OFFICIAL LANGUAGE: ARABIC

You didn't think we've run out of energy superstars to tell you about, did you? Let's talk about the biggest of them all right now—Saudi Arabia!

In the 1930s, Saudi Arabia and an American oil company went on an adventure together. They formed a team called the Arabian American Oil Company, which today is better known by its nickname Aramco.

Guess what? Aramco found a secret treasure—the Ghawar Field, an enormous oil well that just kept giving and giving. Thanks to this awesome find and some top-notch teamwork, Saudi Arabia became the go-to place for countries that need oil (which is almost everyone)!

So next time you're working on a project with your friend, think of the Saudi Arabia story—with strong teamwork and a never-give-up mindset, you can uncover magical things too.

TURKEY

The Car Craftsmen

- POPULATION: 84 MILLION
- CAPITAL: ANKARA
- OFFICIAL LANGUAGE: TURKISH

Ever built a toy car, piece by piece? Now, imagine doing that with real, full-sized car parts! That's Turkey's top talent!

Although Turkey has been making things like textiles and foods for ages, they really revved up their technology game in the 20th century. Under the leadership of their first president, Mustafa Kemal Atatürk, Turkey started to focus more on becoming modern and embracing new technologies.

Today, Turkey is among the top car producers and exporters globally. But what's unique about Turkey's car industry is their expertise in crafting high-quality, innovative car parts that are used in vehicles worldwide, from engines to brakes and more!

Next time you travel to school or the park, remember: a piece of Turkey might be helping you move along! By embracing technology and innovation, Turkey has helped people around the world get to where they need to go!

United Arab Emirates

The Sky-Scraping Sculptors

- Population: 10 million
- Capital: Abu Dhabi
- Official Language: Arabic

Do you like to play with blocks and stack them higher than anyone else? That's what the United Arab Emirates (or UAE for short) loves to do too, but with real materials like steel, glass, and concrete!

Their journey to architectural greatness started in the late 20th century, fueled by oil wealth and the ambition to transform the desert into dazzling cities. Now, the UAE is a massive architectural playground, home to the world's tallest tower, the Burj Khalifa, and many other marvels.

Here's a surprise: some UAE towers are so tall, you can watch the sunset twice—once at the bottom, then again at the top! Incredible, isn't it? The UAE's architectural feats show us that dreaming big can literally elevate our perspectives!

Boys and Girls, Dream BIG!

KA_____

UZ_____

TU____

IR__

IS____

PA_____

SA___ AR____

U__

IN___

SR_ LA___

QUIZ

Can you fill in the names of the countries we discussed on the map? If you need help, feel free to peek at page 8-9!

So____
Ko____
Ja____
Ch____
Ta____
Ph____
Vi____
Th____
Ma____
Si____
In____

Glossary

App

A program on your phone or tablet that lets you do different things, like play games, draw, learn, or chat with friends.

Business

The activity of making, buying, or selling goods or providing services in exchange for money.

Digital

The language that computers and games use to talk to each other. It's how we see pictures and hear sounds on our devices.

Fabric

It's the stuff we use to make clothes or curtains. Think of it as soft paper you can wear or hang up! It comes in all sorts of colors and textures.

Fertilizers

Special plant food that helps them grow tall and strong. It's like vitamins for plants.

Integrated Circuits

Tiny cities of electronics in our devices. They help our toys and gadgets think and work.

Irrigation Canals

Water slides for plants! They help give plants a drink so they don't get thirsty.

Manufacturing

Making things in large amounts, like toys or cars. It's like a big workshop where lots of the same thing get made over and over again.

Outsourcing

Like asking a friend for help. It's giving some tasks to others who are really good at them.

Pesticides

Sprays that keep bugs away from our plants. But be careful! They can also hurt other plants, animals, and even people if not used right.

Process

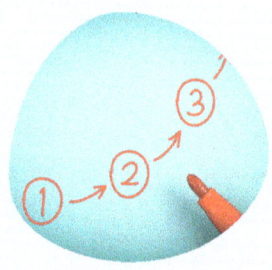

A step-by-step guide that helps you make or find cool things. It's like following a treasure map.

Semiconductor Chips

The brains of our electronics that help our phones, TVs, and other gadgets work.

Streaming

Imagine a show that starts the moment you want it to. No waiting! It's like having a parade of your favorite things on your screen.

Technology

Tools and inventions that make life easier and more fun. With technology, we can do things faster and better.

Transistors

Tiny switches in our gadgets that control the flow of electricity. It's like a traffic cop for electricity in our devices.

Uranium

A special rock from the ground that can make lots of electricity. It's like a powerful battery for our world.

ABOUT THE AUTHOR

Yeonsil Yoo is a children's author and proud mother of a multicultural kid, Yoona, who is Korean, Chinese, American, and Canadian. As a mother and entrepreneur, Yeonsil aspires to teach her daughter not only about her Asian roots, but also real-world lessons, especially about money, business, and worldly perspectives. She wrote this book for her daughter and other curious young minds to help them learn about the real world and nudge them to dream big. To keep updated with her books, visit her website at upflybooks.com or follow her on Instagram @upflybooks.

MORE ADVENTURES AWAIT!

Ready for more adventures?
Embark on a journey to embrace the unfamiliar world!
Available in English and your choice of Chinese, Japanese,
Korean, Tagalog, or Vietnamese!

🛒 **Now Available on Amazon!**

Did you enjoy this adventure? If so, could you please rate this book by leaving some stars on Amazon? Your rating helps other families find this book and lets me create even more exciting journeys for everyone to enjoy!